Life's Funny Ways

Life's Funny Ways

Angela Davis

To order additional copies of this book, contact:
Xlibris Corporation
1-800-618-969
www.Xlibris.com.au
Orders@Xlibris.com.au
501374

Contents

1. Funny Ways 9

In Health

2. How Do You Do...13
3. Packages from Heaven 14
4. Looking for Something 16
5. Exposed 17
6. Making Friends...18
7. Choosing My self..19
8. Take a Leap 21
9. Pride in Mys-elf 23
10. I'm Grumpy..24
11. Knocking on Heavens Door..................................26
12. Playing Tricks..28
13. I Belong to You 29
14. Happiness...31
15. Where Did It Go? 33
16. Sharing You..35
17. Waiting for a Fitting 37
18. Gods Book..39
19. You & I=Me...40
20. Today, is the First Day of the Rest of Your Life.....41
21. Old Flames 43
22. Rock and Roll...45
23. Goodnight, God Bless..47
24. Balance—Baby Steps...48
25. As I Fall..50
26. Unencumbered 52
27. I Surrender to You..54
28. So Much Information 55

29. Habits...57
30. Window to My Soul, or Bottomless Pit? 59
31. My Hat...61
32. Who is there for Me? 62
33. When I'm Ready...64
34. What a Mess! 66
35. My Identity...67
36. Headstrong and Heartfelt...................................69
37. Other Peoples Feelings 71
38. Positively Charged 73
39. Baggage..74
40. Oh Dear, Have You Lost Your Way?...................76
41. Lost Children of God..77
42. My Clumsiness 78
43. Don't Worry...80
44. Looking for You..82
45. Roses in the Park..84
46. God's Little House 86
47. Albert Edward..88
48. My Gift from God 90
49. My Best Friend 92
50. Housework 94
51. Bear and Mouse 96
52. Mighty Mouse 98
53. Tending the Flock 100
54. Bugs and Flu's 101

In Sickness

55. Amazing...105
56. Skin Deep...106
57. Please Hold Me...108
58. Waiting for You to Reply.....................................110
59. Hiding Our Troubles Away 112
60. Intuition 114
61. Hocus Pocus 116
62. Emptiness 117
63. Friends Like You...119
64. Aching for You..121

65. Face Mask 123
66. Gods Cure for Headaches 125
67. Praying to God 127
68. Sick and Tired...128
69. A New Trick...130
70. I've Had Enough!..132
71. Leaving It All Up To You................................134
72. Locked in the Loo!..135
73. Letting My Troubles Go.................................137

UNTIL I RETURN

74. Your love, Is All I Need 141
75. The World is Your Stage................................143
76. No Escape..145
77. Soldiering On 146
78. One Day..147
79. Stairway to Heaven 150
80. On the Road with You 152

1

Funny Ways

God

You have some

Funny ways

Of

Trying to

Get through to me

Remembering

Trusting

Teasing

Laughing

You support me

In

Health

And

In

Sickness

Until

I return

To

You

IN HEALTH

2

How Do You Do

How do You do, what You do?
I'd really like to know
What You do to get through,
And tell me it is so.
You send me lots of messages,
Flying through the air,
Knocking me gently on the head,
To show me You are there.
Can they see what I see too,
Or do they think I'm strange?
Can they hear when I hear You,
Or are You out of range?
What did You do that day,
When You tuned me in?
I'm glad You found the frequency,
I'm glad that I was in.
How do You do, what You do?
I'd really like to know.
There is a button that I know,
I found it in my heart.
I'll push it in and turn it around,
It's the best place to start.

3

Packages from Heaven

Confidence, Faith, Trust and Love.
You sent to me, from Your home above.
You left it, neatly, on my doorstep.
First, I thought it was from a sales rep
Leaving me another tempting sample to try.
I didn't realize, it had come from up High.

I put it away with all the rest.
Shut in a cupboard, I thought I knew best.
I left it shut up, in the dark,
While I want and played in the park.
But, deep inside, I had this feeling.
Not quite knowing, that something was missing.

I remembered the package and went to open it.
But, I'd forgotten where I'd put it.
I turned my house upside down,
By now, I was feeling a bit of a clown.
Because You had given it all to me,
And I'd hidden it away, not wanting to see.

'I give up.' I threw my hands in the air.
'I've searched everywhere, it's just not fair!'
I go to my room and slam the door,
Open the cupboard, don't know what I'm looking for.
But, there it is, just staring at me,
The package from You, that's what I see.

I take it out and then open it up.
'There's lots of Love, for you to fill your cup.
Place your Trust in me, and I'll show you the way
Have Faith, to follow, I won't lead you astray.
You will gain your Confidence, as you speak.
And with all these things, you can start a new week.'

4

Looking for Something

God, I've only got two knees,
And I'm down on them, begging You, 'please'
To help me out and let me see.
To try and find, what's bothering me.
I shout and scream and stomp about.
I go scitzo and yell and shout.
But, underneath it all, you see,
I know that something is bugging me.
It's hidden away, out of my reach.
'Maybe, it's buried on the beach?'
I turn my house, upside down.
And on my face, I have a frown.
'Maybe, it's hiding under a chair?'
I look underneath. 'No, it's not there.'
I empty cupboards. 'Maybe, it's at the back?'
I have to look, for I have the knack
Of storing things up, never throwing them away,
And saving them up, for a rainy day.
I search everywhere. Now I give up,
Cos I even dropped my favourite cup!
Sick and tired, I go to bed.
'Maybe it's all this shit in my head?'

5

Exposed

I'd felt so angry, at being exposed.
From the top of my head, to the tips of my toes.
You stripped me off and left me bare.
'Put it all back on—if you dare.'
I'd felt so good, in the suit I had on.
Then into my life, You came along.
My suit had been a perfect fit,
Then You came and altered it.
It laid in a mess, on the floor.
I jumped over it, to get out the door.
I have some friends, I borrowed their clothes.
But, I don't fit in to those.
So, to the clothes store, off I went.
'Oh, look at these, they are Heaven sent.'
I tried them on, and surprise, surprise!
You should have seen, the look in my eyes.
'It feels so good, what a wonderful fit.
I'll keep it on and wear it today.
It's cold outside and I have to go a long way.'
I raced home and opened the door.
Cleaned up the mess, I didn't need it any more.

6

Making Friends

My ego fights, I get into strife.
Oh, to be myself and live my life.
He never gets tired of being alert.
And tries to protect me, from getting hurt.

But, I'm tired of sitting here, on my own.
It's very lonely, and there's no one else home.
I'd like to get out, and have some fun.
To splash in the rain, and dance in the sun.

So, I'll take a risk and ask him to go.
He'll put up a fight, he might say no.
But, if I persist and ask him again.
He'll see, I'm strong, and go back to his den.

But, it would not be right, to hide him away.
For he is part of me, so I'll ask him to stay.
So, we could hold hands and work together.
And be best friends for ever and ever.

7

Choosing My self

My ego
Is playing up today,
He's getting on my nerves.
He thinks he is cleverer than me,
I don't know who he serves.
He makes noises in my silence,
Puts up a big blank screen.
He thinks he's pretty funny,
Making me angry at his scheme.
But, I know just what he's up to,
So I'll sit here rather calm.
And write down all about him,
I'll set off his own alarm.
Because, I know that in my heart,
He is feeling rather lost.
He's trying to be wanted,
To see who I favour the most.
But, I've got news for him,
That when I decided to be myself.
That I decided, I no longer needed him,
And put him on the shelf.
And there he will stay, forever and a day,
For I know deep in my heart.
That, for myself, I have chosen,
To make a brand new start.
I thank you, ego, for being there,
When you thought I needed you.
But, I know that facing my pain,
Is a choice I make too.
I'm a big girl now, and I can face it,

With Gods help, for,
Myself, I'm strong and full of love,
And God has even more.
I hold His hand and speak to Him,
Every single day.
So, ego, if you're feeling lost,
Ask Him to show you the way.

8

Take a Leap

I'm feeling a sense of foreboding,
For there feels like there is more to come.
I'm right on the edge of something big,
It's an easy hurdle, to jump, for some.

I feel like I should jump right in,
For now there is no holding back
'I've come this far.' I say to You.
'I've already given my ego the sack!'

I had asked him, quietly, to go,
But in the end, I had to stand firm,
And tell him he was no longer needed.
Now, I sit and watch him squirm.

He stands there, too, and laughs at me,
Waiting to see if I fall.
But he does not know, that, I
No longer rely on him at all.

For I have found a special friend,
No conditions does He place on me.
He is there, through thick and thin,
He gives me hugs for free.

So, asking Him to hold my hand,
As I prepare to jump in.
I close my eyes and take a leap,
Fearing what fate might bring.

As I land, with a splash,
I know I have done right.
I jump up and down, excited,
Amazed at this wonderful sight.

For, there, underneath my feet,
Is a puddle, full of fun.
I splash around and make a mess,
It's the best thing I have ever done.

I start to laugh, I'm dripping wet,
But I don't care at all.
For I'm having fun with You.
'Please, next, can we play ball?'

9

Pride in Mys-elf

I'm starting to understand the different sorts of pride.
One, is so open and loving, the other, is an attempt to hide.
No wonder I grew up so confused, about loving myself,
I did not know the difference between a goblin and an elf.
For a goblin lives under the ground and hides in the dark alleyway.
And sneaks around, pretending and tries to frighten others away.
He thinks he is strong, big and tough, and can do anything at all.
When, really, he does not see very well and hurts himself when he falls.
But, being a stubborn little goblin, he gets up and pretends he's alright.
He jumps around and frightens you and he tucks his hurt out of sight.

But, on the other hand, a little elf is sweet and full of love.
You would not even know he's there, until he gives you a gentle shove.
And says to you, that 'you did well', and, he is 'very proud'.
He whispers this to you, inside your heart, for he is not very loud.
He is quite shy and is content to encourage you, in this way.
To tell you he loves you, for trying your best and doing so well on this
day.
So, now I'm not scared anymore, of saying 'I love myself',
For I know, that deep inside my heart, it is my little elf.
And if my goblin ever comes out and wants to play with me,
I ask him 'why he's hurt?' And, I can help, if he lets me see.

Because if I'm open and loving and make no attempt to hide,
I can be really proud of myself, instead of hurting my pride.

10

I'm Grumpy

Why am I so God dam grumpy?
The bed's unmade, the custard's lumpy.
I've got a pain, here, in my foot.
I cannot run, 'oh bugger it!'

I swear and curse, all day long.
Nothing is right, it's all gone wrong.
My perceptions have turned, upside down.
Now, instead of a smile, I wear a frown.

For my world of make believe,
Is lost forever, so I grieve.
For a world that was so fake,
Now, I know, my fate, You make.

For I can choose, which path I take.
But, in the end, You will give me a shake.
And ask me. 'Where am I going to—
Living in hell, or walking with You?'

My stubborn pride, throws a tantrum.
Stamps its foot, acts like it's dumb.
For it knows, deep down inside,
That there is nowhere it can hide.

That it is time, to move on.
That life is evolving, the past is gone.
It is time, to live and be free,
With faith in my heart, to be me.

It feels left out, so it has a hissy fit.
I think I'll watch and humour it.
Give it some space, to calm down.
I laugh, as it acts like a clown.

It cheers me up,
As I sit back and see.
Remembering, accepting,
You are a part of me.

11

Knocking on Heavens Door

It was a bit of a shock to me,
When I found out.
That I had forgotten my key
And I had locked myself out.
I tried to climb in through the window,
But, I got stuck.
The spare key was not there,
I was running out of luck.
I'd stayed out late and I thought,
'I'd be in lots of trouble now.'
For I'd have to knock loudly
And wake You up, somehow.
It was cold outside, but I stood there,
Wondering what to do.
For if I woke You in the middle of the night,
Would You be angry too?
'Please, God, can You help me?'
For I'm feeling very scared.
I want to get back inside
And I did not come prepared.
I forgot my key, the spare one's gone,
So I knock, quietly, on the door.
Then I sit down on the step. 'What else can I do?'
I've never done this before.
The door opened, slowly, and then to my surprise,
You stood there.
With arms open wide, saying. 'Come on in,
Did you not think, I would care?
For I'm always waiting,
I never sleep, until you're all home.

For I love all my children,
I never rest until you come.
I wait patiently,
Until, I hear you all gently knock.
For everyone forgets their key, to the door,
They need to unlock.'
'Oh, thank You, God, for waiting here,
For me, so patiently.'
I say, as we share a great big hug,
As I sit upon His knee.

12

Playing Tricks

I love the way You play tricks on me
Just checking, making sure I still see.

You take all the handles off my mugs,
To let me know that You give me hugs.

For when I'm left, with just two,
There's only one mug for me, and one, for You.

You stop me going backwards, any way You can.
You even break my ankle, when, from You, I ran.

So I had to listen, for, I could not even walk.
You really left me no choice, boy, can You talk!

And when I want some silence, there's lots of noise around
You test my patience, when I'm looking for what I've found.

For Your love, for me, is everywhere I look.
And even when I don't, You pop up in a book!

I hope one day, that I learn to understand,
How to stay one step ahead, of the tricks You have planned

To teach me, all that I need, to live life with You.
Then, maybe, I'll reach Heaven and play a trick on You.

13

I Belong to You

Where do I come from?
And where do I belong?
In looking for the answer,
I didn't think it would take me long.
All I had to do, was find out
When and where I was born.,
And the names of my parents.
So, why was I so forlorn?
That the answers I was given,
Did not seem quite right, to me.
So, I had to keep on searching,
There was more, there just had to be.
I looked in many places,
Some were dusty, some were very dark.
I even took the dog for a walk,
Thinking, I might find the answer in the park.
I ran out of places, where I thought
I would find the answer to my problem.
I got quite exhausted,
Maybe, I had just got it all wrong!
I took a book down to the beach
And sat down in the silence.
For, I thought, I would let the sea air
Clear my head of all this nonsense.
It was there that I found the answer,
As the wind whispered to me.
As the waves gently greeted the sand,
Everything seemed so free.
I sat in wonder, as I realized
What had been there all the time.

The answer to my question had been there,
Waiting in the sunshine
For me to listen to the whispering wind,
For me to open my eyes wide,
For me to sit in the silence,
So that I could know—the answers are inside
My heart, where You have written it all,
And all I need to do is look
To find out that I am Your child, I belong to You,
You wrote it in a book.
All I have to do is to open it up
And start to read it for myself.
Then I will be free to feel Your love,
Instead of sitting forlorn on the shelf.

14

Happiness

Where did I go and hide
All my happiness?
I'd like to find it again,
For I really miss
Looking in the mirror,
At the smile on my face.
I wish I could remember,
For I need to find that place
And put the feeling back,
Where it does belong.
For I've got something missing
And it feels all wrong.
I think I put it away,
In a drawer one day,
When a few responsibilities
Decided to stay.
I put it there
For I needed some time, to sort out
What was going to stay,
And what I was throwing out.
But, then I forgot which drawer
I had put it in.
I was really sure
I hadn't put it in the bin.
I think I had better find it
Really, really soon.
For I'm getting pretty angry
And it's not a full moon.
So I can't blame it
On the universe today.

For I was the one
Who hid my happiness away.
And forgot to get it out,
When I had finally decided
What responsibilities were mine,
And those I abided.
And handed them back
To whom they did belong,
Discovering, to my surprise,
That I was really strong.
So, now I'm asking my strength,
To help me find
The happiness, that's stuck in the drawer,
That I left behind.

15

Where Did It Go?

I feel like all the fun,
Has been squeezed out of my life.
I don't know where it has gone to,
Did it get cut out by a knife?
For I have this pain,
Where I know my fun should be.
I wish I knew where it has gone?
I think it is hiding from me.
I'm feeling so sad, for I think,
That I have lost it somewhere.
Maybe, I left it on a shelf?
Maybe, it hid, when I tore out my hair?
Did my fun get scared,
When I got mad and decided to go away?
Or, did it think that I did not care,
When I lost it and chose not to stay?
I really wish that I knew,
So that I could put it back
Where it belongs, for this pain
I feel, is starting to get the knack
Of hurting me, when I'm already down,
And I need cheering up.
So, where on earth is the fun,
That used to fill my cup?
For I cannot replace it
With something that may be false.
I really need to find it and then,

Maybe, I could learn to waltz
With You and have a laugh,
As we dance in the midday sun.
For I'm really missing being stupid
And having lots of fun.

16

Sharing You

When I woke this morning,
I had a feeling You were mad at me.
What it was all about,
That, I just could not see.
I don't have to get up just yet,
So I think I'll stay in bed.
For all this stuff is just going round
And round in my head.
Do this, do that, shut up, sit down,
I wish they'd go away.
I don't think this is turning out,
To be a very good day.
You're mad at me, and I know You are,
So I want to stay here and hide.
Is it that I went out without You,
And You stayed home and cried?
I did not leave You home all alone,
For I really had You with me.
I held You closely in my heart,
Where no one else could see.
Is that why You are mad at me,
Because I kept You all to myself?
Instead of sharing the love I have for You,
And telling everyone else,
That there is only one true love,
That I hold, deep in my heart.
And if I keep Him in there,
We will never be far apart.
But, I just forgot to remember,
That I still need to let others know

That I have a love for You,
That's above all else, and to start to show,
How beautiful You are to the rest of the world,
And not to hide my love away.
Not to keep You all to myself, for You
Have a love that grows, stronger every day.
And it would not be fair to You,
For You would miss out on all the fun
And love that there is in my life,
Now, that with You, it has just begun.

17

Waiting for a Fitting

You waited for me for such a long time, I'm so glad that You did.
For if You didn't, I'd still be lost, in the place where I had hid.
I'd still be sad, feeling so lost and alone without You.
I'm so glad that You came along and said. 'How do you do.'
For I wasn't doing very well, even though I thought I was.
I was stuck in a rut, too scared to move and blaming everyone, because

I didn't want to look at myself, for what if I found something there
That I would have to alter? What was wrong with my clothes and my hair?
I was perfect, I was so slim, I dressed in all the best clothes,
I wouldn't be seen dead in a tracksuit—only losers wore those.
For they hide your body away from view, how can you show the real you,
That everyone can plainly see, when you wear clothes that fit tight to you?

I must admit I got it wrong, maybe, I should eat my hat!
For I sat here in my ivory tower, saying. 'How on earth could they wear that?'
For I did not see, did not want to know, that it's what's inside that matters.
I'd quietly thought, to myself, that they were as mad as hatters.
I did not stop and think, until You had asked me how I was doing,
For You were the One, who noticed that all my seams, had started undoing.

And I could not keep in, all the things that I was trying to hide from view.
You took me aside and quietly said to me. 'May I be of service to you,
I think you need some help, to show the world what you have inside.
It's much too beautiful to keep locked away, you don't have to hide.
You don't have to wear this suit, that keeps everything perfectly tucked in.
So lets let it all out and then we'll choose something comfortable, lets begin.

But first of all, why not relax and take off those tight clothes,
Put on this tracksuit, it's nice and loose, much more comfortable than those.
See how you can walk around, it's a style that's easy to fit.
There's a mirror over there, why don't you take a look in it?'
I feel so free, it feels so good to finally find something that I fit in to.
'Thank You so much for all Your help, I could never have done it without You.'

18

Gods Book

I no longer give myself away, to everyone I see.
For what they see is what they get, this is the true me.
They might not like what they get, but, it is up to them to choose
To take what they see and figure out if it's true, or You they lose.

It only takes a little time, to stop, so silently and look
Inside at their hearts, open them up and read them, like a book.
For every page is different and we can read a new one every day.
It breaks my heart to see though, if they choose to lock it away.

My heart is an open book, I choose to read it all of the time.
It's so much fun, I run and jump, laugh and cry, just like in a pantomime.
For God wrote the script, for life's play and it's inside us, if we look.
I chose to raise the curtain, jump on stage and live life by the book.

The critics can be very harsh and their opinions are, just that.
And I know, so on with the show, today I'm going to act like a cat
That rests all day, curled up in someone's lap, while they gently stroke my fur.
They give me milk to drink, say 'what a beautiful girl' and I'm in Heaven,
I purr.

It's not hard to figure out that all of life is just a stage,
The way we act, the way we play, it doesn't matter what our age.
For when we love what we do, where we may be and who we are,
Life is true for me and you. We are in Heaven. We're truly a star.

19

You & I=Me

You
You had a dream that one day your prince would come.
Your knight inn shining armour and he would rescue you from
The life you lived, that in your own way,
You thought you'd like to escape from, rather than stay
And face your fears, so that you could be free,
To travel your journey along the road, with Me.

You found your prince and them married him.
Then one by one, added children to your dream.
But, like all dreams, in the end we awake
To face the reality of the life, that we must make,
To find the freedom, that is within our heart,
To face our fears and make a new start.

I
I woke up one day and threw back the cover.
No longer able to be the perfect wife and mother.
I couldn't explain and didn't know where to start.
All I know, is that it was breaking my heart.
I'd lost myself, somewhere along the way.
I had to try and find me, I could not stay.

I looked around, but there were so many faces.
I even tried to hide, in the darkest places.
I went out of my mind and started to find,
That inside my heart, there was the right kind
Of place, to seek the child that was me.
Who was waiting patiently, and sitting on Your knee.

20

Today, is the First Day of the Rest of Your Life

Thank You God for giving me the icing on the cake.
When someone said I could have it, I thought there had been some mistake.
I had my cake already. Was I allowed to eat it too?
I'd always been taught not to ask for too much from You.
It had not seemed fair that I could not ask for anything at all,
For those who asked did not get, while others had it all!
So when they said I could have it all, I had a doubt or two.
For it would mean that I had to ask, for something from You.
I swallowed my pride and took a chance, curiosity got the better of me.
For I had to go check out for myself, what was plain for all to see.
So, without revealing too much at all, in the darkness, I arrived.
It was cold and wet, I was so afraid, that I admit, I cried.
I tried to run away that night, but, I'd left my boots at home.
I was stuck with You, in the wilderness, with nowhere else to roam.
I sneezed, I coughed, I got cold feet, this place was making me sick,
But You reached out and held my hand, You were as solid as a brick.
You held me close, in my time of need, and You listened patiently.
Waiting for me to overcome my fear and pour out all my troubles,
that You see.
So tenderly, You wiped my brow, saying. 'Suffer no more in silence.'
You held me close and whispered in my ear.
'There will be no more violence,
It's safe to come out now, you've been living, long enough,
in your own private hell.'
You stay with me and hug me tight, telling me. 'That you'll protect me
forever as well.
That all I had to do was ask, that You would not turn me away.
That You would always be there, whether it was night or it was day.'

To hear You say those words to me, meant more that I can ever say.
For when I'd asked You for Your help, You were there, in every way.
You held me, hugged me, touched my hand, picked me up and bathed
me too.
Without ever asking, You gave it all to me, when all I'd done was hidden
from You.
I realized what they said, when I could have my cake and eat it too.
For what we see inside, is what we get, and what I found inside
me—was You.
Curiosity may have killed the cat, but this one got the cream.
Now I jump up and down for joy and from all the rooftops scream—
Would you like to ice your cake, I know a very good supplier.
His door is always open to you and His shelves could be stacked no higher.
Just go inside and take a look, because you'll be amazed at what you see.
There's lots of love, and then there's trust, there's lots of faith in there too.
And if you can fid the courage, there are big hearts in here for you.
There is lots more, and it's all inside a place, that I visit every day,
It's God's House you see, just ask Him and He will show you the way.

21

Old Flames

When I say 'I love You',
I feel the warmth inside my heart.
There is a special place, at the centre,
Where it lights a flame, to start
A glow, that just gets brighter,
With every breath that I take.
It makes me feel all fuzzy inside
And no excuses, will I make.
It's Your love inside my heart,
That's waited there for me.
Your flame was always there,
Just flickering and hoping I would see.
It never gave up hope, that one day
I would look inside
And notice something different,
That You, had never attempted to hide.
But I had thought something was burning me,
And tried to put it out.
You always had faith, that I would see,
You never had any doubt.
You kept it burning, even when I locked up my heart
And thought I'd lost the key.
You nurtured and protected my flame,
For You always had faith in me.
So, from one old flame to another,
I'm so glad You took the time
And held on to Your faith in me,

Especially when I had lost mine.
I love You so much, I hope You know,
It feels so warm inside of me.
I'm so glad You are a bright spark
And looked after my key.

22

Rock and Roll

I've got this feeling, in my heart
That goes deep, in to my soul.
The only way I can describe it,
Is to call it 'Rock and Roll'.
It makes me want to move around,
And then, I start to wriggle.
It fills my heart with laughter
And then I start to giggle.
For life is so much fun today,
My heart is doing a dance.
So take my hand, lets fool around,
Have fun, just take a chance.
For we are young and free, you see,
But we only have one life
To be who we are in this time,
Even if we are man and wife.
For when we say 'I do' to You,
We then start to realize,
That in all our foolish wisdom,
We had closed our eyes.
We say 'I do' to each other,
Giving our hearts away.
We forget to keep our promise
To live, with You, each day.
We sell our soul to the Devil,
Who just hates to dance.
We gave ourselves away that day,

When we took a chance,
Thinking that this was our true love,
We locked away our soul.
And forgot that the meaning of life
Is to Rock and Roll.

23

Goodnight, God Bless

In the middle of the night,
I sometimes wake up and think.
I cannot get back to sleep,
Until I've had a drink.
I lay there, wide awake you know,
The thoughts go round in my head.
Maybe I may get back to sleep,
If I eat some bread.
My thirst is quenched, my tummy's full,
But, still I do not sleep.
I start to get frustrated, but then,
Remember to count sheep.
I get to over one hundred,
Before it really dawned on me
That I had forgotten to say goodnight,
To someone who loves me.
I get out of bed and kneel right down,
And quietly say to You.
'Goodnight God, I'm sorry, I forgot,
I hope I didn't wake You too.
For I could not settle until I've thanked You,
For being with me today.
For sending me lots of love,
And special things, to help me find my way.
So goodnight, God Bless,
I hope that You can feel my love for You.
And keep it in a special place,
With the candle, I light for You too.'

24

Balance—Baby Steps

I'm finding it hard to keep my balance,
It is really bothering me.
Where am I going wrong? What is there, I do not see?
I fall over backwards,
I wobble to and fro.
I feel like giving up,
Not getting on with the show.
What am I scared of?
What do I need to set me free?
Why can't I relax
And just let things be?
Am I trying too hard to see,
What is right before my very eyes?
Will You please help me?
Do You hear my desperate cries?
For I know I have to work it out,
If I am to succeed.
If I am to move forward,
Will You help me in my hour of need?
Why do I falter?
Why do I hesitate and lose my step?
I wish I could find my balance,
I wonder where it is kept?
Did I give it away one day,
Or just put it somewhere safe?
Did I ever have it to begin with?
Is it lost, like a little waif?
Is that why I do not have it,
Or am I looking for something I have not got?
I'll need to take some baby steps,

Or I may fall out of my cot.
I will keep on trying,
For I know, I can get up, if I am down.
I have determination,
It's not really a frown.
I know that I can do it,
I just need to practice and take my time.
And if I get a little stuck,
I know that I'm
Held by You, I cannot fall,
You're holding me very tight.
Giving me confidence,
Your strength and all Your might.
I just need to hold on to You,
And trust that it will all be okay.
Put myself into Your hands, and know,
That You will guide me—all the way.

25

As I Fall

My legs just seem to hang there,
At the bottom of my bum.
Why do thy seem to act,
Like they are quite dumb?
Well, they just don't seem to know,
Just what to do.
They wobble and they wibble,
When I try to walk to You.
You say, to me, to just let go,
Put one foot in front of the other.
But, they just seem to tangle up
And trip over one another.
I feel so uncoordinated,
Just like a duck out of water.
I just can't seem to move,
Like I know I ought to.
Do I have some lines crossed,
So I get all mixed up?
Or, am I just clumsy, each time I fall,
As I trip up?
Maybe, I should just sit still
For a while and rest.
Gather up my strength again,
Try to wait and see what is best.
Enjoy the warmth and the laughter,
As I sit with You.
Then try, this time, to walk, listening,
As You instruct me in what to do.
Trusting that You will be there,
Each time I fall to the ground.

For it is okay to make a mistake,
And sometimes go round and round
In circles, as I try
To regain my balance, as I falter.
For You hold the reins to my life in Your hands,
That, will never alter.
So it is safe, for me, to take a risk,
To let go and have some fun.
For You will always be there,
Laughing, with me, as I fall on my bum.

26

Unencumbered

Nothing seems to fit,
It's either too tight or too small.
Too baggy, or too big,
I can't find anything at all.
I try this, I buy that,
It fits for a while.
Then, I am happy,
You can tell by my smile.
But, before too long,
It seems to alter its shape,
I might as well cover myself up,
With a big black cape!
And disappear from view,
So no one has to look
At the sight before them,
Or pretend to read a book,
When they see me walking by,
Ashamed to say 'hello'
Not wanting to acknowledge,
That it is me they know.
I think, I will have a sort out,
Of all that does not fit.
Give it away to someone else,
I'm sure they could make use of it.
Mental, physical or emotional,
I'll clean it out.,
So that my mind, body and spirit,

Are free to move about,
Without any discomfort,
In any shape or form today,
Able to express my being,
In a totally unencumbered way.

27

I Surrender to You

It hurts when I ignore my feelings,
When I do not acknowledge my self.
So, why is it that I end up battered and bruised,
Before I remember to listen?
I carry on, in my own little world,
Falling over my own two feet.
I walk into walls, I bump my head,
Then I give myself concussion?
Maybe I try to knock myself out,
So that I do not have to face reality.
So that I have an excuse to run away,
From all things that cause me pain.

But, this time, I forgot to put on a coat,
Pack a case, or take an umbrella with me.
Now I'm exposed and cold, for you all to see,
My emotions are caught in the rain.
Unprotected and vulnerable, I stand strong, in my faith,
With You by my side.
Willing to face all that is in front of me,
I wait and listen to Your voice.
My ego, too weak to argue,
My self, ready to acknowledge all that I feel.
Ready to surrender, to Your will,
To move forward, on the path of Your choice.

28

So Much Information

Incoming—so many messages, I'll never get it right.
'You have mail.' So much to sort out, I don't feel very bright.
Snowed under a mountain of information to absorb today.
Maybe, I'll pretend to be someone else, hope it will all go away.

But the knocking gets louder, until I open the door.
The telephone keeps ringing, there's mail all over the floor!
It's not going to go away, I have to sort it all out.
No one else, but me, knows what these messages are about.

For they are meant for me alone, to help me on my journey.
Until I stop and listen to them, I will never really be free.
They will keep on piling up, I will become snowed under.
If I continue to take no notice, Your voice will roar like thunder.

For You have tried every which way, You can, to talk to me.
And You are only trying to help me, the way ahead, to see,
Before I break down, crushed by the load, that I carry around.
Absorbing all, not filtering out, it weighs heavily, crushes, without a
sound.

Yet, my life could be so simple, if only I stopped and listened to You.
For You are only trying to ask me, if You can help carry my burdens too.
The thoughts and fears, opinions of others, actions and words that maim.
The pathways, that I've taken alone, the untold guilt and shame.

That You understand, that You forgive, for there is no sin, in Your eyes.
You understand, that I am here to learn, that, with You, I cannot disguise
The real me, the truth inside, the love, that will always be
Forever in my heart for You, when I open my mail, I will see

That with You by my side, when I listen,
You lighten my load.
The mountains I climb are beautiful,
As I walk, with You, down the road.

29

Habits

I have these little habits,
Do they irritate you?
Cos, sometimes, I get a bit annoyed,
With myself, too.
I try to be just like me,
But, sometimes, I just am
Upside down and clumsy,
Just like a newborn lamb.
I stumble around and make mistakes,
Without even trying.
But, this is me, so there is no use in trying,
To cover up, by lying.
I trip up and fall over,
My very own two feet.
I always drop things down me,
I don't look very neat.
Tissues, somehow, get in the wash,
Though I've cleaned all my pockets.
When I laugh and cry,
My eyeballs bulge in their sockets.
I'd forget my head,
If it was not screwed on,
Though in the end,
I really think I have won.
For I am me,
You get, all that you see.
When I laugh, until I cry,
Then I need to pee.
Whites, that turn pink,
Burnt dinners—I haven't a clue!

Messages you can write, in the dust,
To name but a few.
A well worn old car,
That needs a good clean.
If it did, would it fall apart?
You know what I mean!
Weeds that grow tall,
The garden is like a nature reserve.
An expression of me—
What a learning curve!
Full of surprises,
Around every corner that you turn,
A child, in Gods playground,
Here, to learn.

30

Window to My Soul, or Bottomless Pit?

Why do I feel like my brain has just flown out of the window?
For my mind is not clear and does not remember what it should know.
It is all fogged up and everything seems to be as clear as mud
That has all dried up and just looks like a pile of crud,
That is taking up so much space, but, seems too hard to move.
I think I need an excavator, for the situation to improve!
Because I tried to pick it up, but, it just would not budge.
Then, I tried to move it sideways, with a great big nudge!
But, it just sat there, ignoring me and refused to move at all.
So, now I need a warning sign, in case I trip over it and fall.

Because, if I fall and bumped my head, then I might forget
What it was that I had to do and I don't want to do that, just yet.
For I have to find a way, to clear this fog, right out of my mind.
Then I might remember and be amazed at what I may find
In my brain, for I know, that it has a lot of information
That may be useful, to me, so maybe, I will send it an invitation
To step inside my mind today and find clear words, that may be spoken.
And ask it to look out for a window, that, maybe, I can open
To let some fresh air in today, that might blow the fog away.
Because, I think, it has got quite settled and is determined to stay.

For sitting right in front of it, there appears to be a big black hole.
Maybe, this is what I am looking for, the window to my soul.
And, if the fog got cleared away, then I might be able to see
What was at the other end of the big black hole. Would I then be free?
To move around and not worry about, falling over any mess.

For there would be a space in my head, or would there just be less
For me to have to worry about, so my way would become clear
To look into the big black hole, when I've overcome my fear
That it really is a bottomless pit and I may never be able to get out of it.
Instead of getting clearer, I will have just landed my self in the shit!

31

My Hat

I thought I had been there and done that
But, all I had done, was put on a different hat
It was not mine, it was borrowed from a sort of friend
But, it suited me to wear it, I thought I would—until the end.

But, we all know what thought did, this time it got it wrong..
Even though the thought stayed, until a gust of wind came along.
It blew everything out of proportion, I was just like a mad hatter,
For I liked the simple life, I wanted the former—not the latter.

But, no matter how hard I tried, the hat just would not fit back on.
I even turned it inside out, but, my thoughts no longer, did belong.
For they were borrowed from a friend, now, it was time to give them
back.
It was time to find my own hat, be brave, and defend against attack.

For my friends did not like it, when I returned a hat. that would no
longer fit.
For they still thought it suited me and were offended—quite a bit.
I did say I was sorry, but, I thought they needed it themselves,
And I was going to get a new one, maybe, Peter Pans, or an elves.

I was going to have fun, trying on lots of different styles.
And maybe, one day, I would find a few, even if I had to travel for miles.
So, I'm sorry if I offended anyone, by standing up for myself.
But, I much prefer being me, a mischievous little elf!

32

Who is there for Me?

As much as I'd like to think,
That I can handle things on my own.
I'd really like some help, sometimes,
So I reach for you, on the phone
For you are not with me, and
I need to talk to you right now.
So, as I dial your number,
I hope this message will reach you, somehow.
For you are unavailable, the message says
You cannot answer the phone.
So, does this mean that I will have to deal with this,
All on my own?
I look up to the Heavens, and
Once more I pray to God,
Hoping that this message might reach Him,
As I slowly nod
My head, when I realize, that He
Is always there for me.
Even when, at times, it is not always
Plain for me to see.
Because I'd like to think,
That I can handle everything by myself.
But even Santa had lots of helpers,
Like Rudolf and the elves.
So God, I'm asking You today,
If it is possible, at all, to send
Some help, to get through this?
For it feels like I'm going around the bend!
For I help everyone else,
When they have troubled times in their life.

But, where are they all, when I'm calling for help,
And in strife?
Why is it, that the only one available to me,
In my hour of need?
Is You, God in Heaven above,
Now that I have been freed
From all things in my life,
That hold me to the material worth.
So, did I forget to call You up,
Before I phoned a friend, here on earth?
Is that why, in my times of crisis
And my emotions are racing fast,
That You arrange it, so that I talk to You first,
And them last?

33

When I'm Ready

I'm angry at something and
I don't know what it is.
So, how can I get rid of it?
It has got me in a tiz.
For the more I try to see,
What it is I can find,
The more I think I must be,
Slowly, going blind.
So, now I need to sit still,
And think for a while.
Because when I'm angry,
I forget how to smile.
And I really think,
That I would prefer to have some fun,
Than send myself mad,
Being angry with someone.
So please God, listen,
I really need some help, today.
I'd like to send this anger somewhere else,
If I may?
I know I'm not being very polite,
At all, to You.
But, when I'm very angry,
I lose all my p's and q's.
It's no excuse, I know,
And I'm really very sorry
That I'm in such a state,
It really is a worry.
I wish I knew just what to do,
With all of it today.

For I know I cannot,
Just let it all sit, in this way.
I have to find out,
So that I can let it all go.
So, if You have any ideas,
Can You please let me know?
I'll sit here in the silence,
For it is best that I don't talk.
Cos, every time that I open my mouth,
My brain goes for a walk!
So, thank You, God, for listening,
As I ramble, on and on.
I know that when I'm ready, Your reply,
Will not take long.
So, until that time, that I hear from You,
I'll wait patiently.
So that I will be ready, for Your answer,
And I will see.

34

What a Mess!

Every time I panic,
I know I should sit back and wait.
And have a good look at the mess, I think,
Instead of getting in a state.
For every time that I dive straight in and say
'It looks okay to me'
The mess just gets worse,
For I am in the middle and cannot see
That all around me, if I look,
Is the mess that I created, myself,
By leaving things to the last minute,
Or hiding them on the shelf
To wait until I thought I would have the time,
To sort them out.
Knowing, that I should have done it then,
For most of it, I could have thrown out!
For most of the mess does not belong to me,
I borrowed it, from a friend.
And now there's lots of things here, that are broken
And I'm trying to mend
Before I give it back, to the friend
That I borrowed it from that day.
For it would not be very nice to return it all,
In an even messier way.
Because, then I would not be sorting it all out,
I'd just be giving it all to you.
So, I think I need to sit back and sort out,
What is mine and what is yours,
Then I can sort out my own mess,
And give myself a round of applause.

35

My Identity

In the search for my identity,
My journey took me far.
From one end of the earth, to the other,
I looked in every bar.
I found nothing,
At the bottom of the glass.
All I ever did—
Was to fall and land on my ass!
Being that close to the ground,
I sifted through the dirt.
All that ever did—
Was to make my knees hurt!
When I could not walk,
I buried my head in the sand.
For I was too stubborn,
To ask for a helping hand.
So, cold and lonely, hurting
And with a head full of shit,
I stayed where I was,
Too scared to move—for a bit.
I lied, I cheated myself,
Into believing I was alive.
When in reality—
I was struggling to survive.
I almost killed myself,
With my own ignorance.
It led me in circles—
A very merry dance!
Tired and alone,
With my head spinning around,

I reached out to You,
Then, without a sound,
You held me close, like a newborn babe,
In Your arms.
You showed me life, through Your eyes,
Using Your worldly charms—
Angels, in disguise, protecting me,
As I grew up.
Until I could walk and talk,
Drink from my own cup.
Then You took my hand
And led me to a special place,
Where I could look inside,
And come face to face
With myself, and take a chance—
On who I may see.
Get to know and love—
My real identity!

36

Headstrong and Heartfelt

There is something inside my head, it does not want to let go.
But it has gone past the date, that says, that it is so.
It says that the time has come, that it is no longer useful.
So, it is time to move on, but it is still trying to pull
Me back to the place where I used to live, a long time ago.
The place inside my head, where everything—it used to know.
But times, they change, and so can we, if we really want to.
The only dilemma that we have, is that, we need to change two.

First, our heart and then our head, or is it the other way around?
Either way, it makes no difference, as long as they are both found
To agree on what was decided, which was the best path, for them to take.
But, if they choose to disagree, then it's a difficult choice to make.
For they struggle to control the person, that we think we are,
And try to protect us in the way, that has worked for them, so far.

Our hearts contain the truth and feel for us, every step of the way.
Our minds try to take over and rationalize, everything that we say.
And when they work together, letting each one take their turn,
They help us to grow up and protect us, while in this life, we learn.
But, sometimes, the balance of the two of them, gets a bit upset.
Especially when a tragedy occurs, or so headstrong, we get.

Then it takes a while to mend a broken heart, or relax the mind.
For they are feeling lost and alone and are stumbling along blind
To the place, where they go when they are feeling this way.
Where they take their time and rest, but, sometimes want to stay.
In the safety that they have found inside my head, or locked inside my heart.
So, here I am again, inside my head, trying to make a start
And ask it, to just let go, for I am no longer in any danger.
For my heart has found the way home, and is no longer frightened of the stranger.

37

Other Peoples Feelings

Other peoples feelings,
Seem to get in the way.
Quite uninvited,
They settle in and stay!
They barge through the door,
Even if it is closed.
Not waiting to be asked,
Or answer any question that is posed.
They rudely ignore,
Any polite suggestions to go.
For they think they are better,
Than any feelings we know.
They stubbornly sit,
Refusing to budge an inch.
While we timidly wait,
Then remember the winch.
For with some help,
We can prise them out of their seat
We can give them a thought,
Thank them for the chance to meet.
And while they are still thinking,
Just how to reply.
We can stand up tall and look them
Squarely in the eye.
Say. 'Thank you for the time
And the trouble that you took
But all of your feelings,
Belong in your own book.
It is nice to know, that you,
Would like to share them with me

But, I have my own book too,
Would you like to see?
They are my feelings
And I understand that if you
Choose to ignore them,
For I know, that you are too
Set in the habit of thinking,
You are more important than me.
So, thank you for visiting,
But, you are really free
To go back to the place,
Where you truly belong,
The heart of your creator,
To stay would be wrong.
For you are not mine,
You are needed in your own home
You belong to your creator,
Together, you may roam.'

.

38

Positively Charged

God, am I glad that I got all of that crap out of the way.
For it would have made me mad, if it had decided to stay.

Because I'd held on to it, for long enough and it was rather tiring.
So I'm glad that it agreed with me and decided to do some rewiring.

For the stuff inside my head, had been negative for far too long.
And when I tried to ground myself, I would end up getting it all wrong.

For I would go shopping for some new clothes, makeup, or a book.
When I really needed to take a walk on the beach, or take a look.

At the flowers in the park, the trees and the birds and the bees.
And let the earth take all my worries, and carry them away on the breeze.

Then I could look at life more positive, for there would be nothing in my head
That would take charge and just demand, overloading, so I would dread

To switch on in the morning, for my brain was already full up.
And it was getting into such a mess, that I was dribbling, like a pup

So now there is space to move around, without getting my wires crossed
Since I decided to sort out and all my troubles, they were tossed.

Away, forever, into the night, where they can spark continually, out there.
Using the energy that they have, light the way and positively share

With the world, all the energy available to us that we can use.
Instead of storing away what we don't need, until we end up blowing a fuse.

39

Baggage

Hey, that's my suitcase, full of clothes.
Don't take it away, I need all of those.
I'm going on a journey that won't take long
But, I'll take spare shoes, for I could be wrong.
As I travel on, slowly, down the road
I add some more things, to my load.
I'm young and strong, it seems so easy,
I don't notice that I'm getting wheezy.

I cram in everything I can find.
Not wanting to leave anything behind.
It gets so full, I sit on it.
So determined, that everything will fit.
Friends, they say, 'I've got something for you,
And while it's open, put this in there too.'
'Hold on a minute, my back is sore,
I don't want to carry this, anymore!'

I open it up and look inside.
God, it's scary, I run and hide.
I lock it away for another week,
Then, I come back and take a peek.
There's too much here for me to carry about.
I think that I'll just throw it all out.
But, how can I get rid of all of this?
Everything is in here that, I think, I would miss.

Then, one day, it just exploded!
God, that case was really loaded.
I had to deal with the mess that was inside.
I wanted to run, but, I couldn't if I tried.
I was stuck in it, right up to my eyes,
And first, I had to sort out all of those ties.
Then the shoes, that did not fit.
The shirt off my back, it's a bottomless pit!

Underneath it all, I came across
An outfit, I'd thought had been no great loss.
This was the one I could not give away.
So I put it on, and I wear it today.
I emptied the case and threw it away.
For this is the way, I would like to stay.
And I'll travel my journey, barefoot and free.
Showing the world, that this is me!

40

Oh Dear, Have You Lost Your Way?

Oh dear me, what is the matter with you?
Anyone would think you had lost your shoe.
What are you standing there like that for?
Why don't you come on in and shut the door?

You look like you may have lost your way.
Are you too scared to open your mouth and say
What you want and why you are here?
Is there something here, that you fear?

Now, speak up child, there is no need to mumble,
As you are standing there, looking very humble,
For I will not shout and bite your head off.
Is there something that I can give you for your cough?

I have some medicine here for you
So open your mouth, it tastes horrible—true.
But it will help you to get better.
So let us follow the instructions—to the letter.

It says to take it twice a day, at least.
And rest for a while, so that you can enjoy the peace
And listen to what your heart has to say.
For it thinks you are lost, and it knows the way.

41

Lost Children of God

You found me wandering down the road and gently took my hand.
'Are you lost, little girl? Can you remember where you are from?'
You sat me down upon Your knee and found a box of tissues
To wipe my eyes and blow my nose. 'Now, have you lost your mum?'

I sat and pondered, for a while, the thoughts ran through my head.
'I've run away again,' I said 'I really don't like living there.
But I think I've lost my way, because this place looks rather strange.
I'm feeling very frightened and this place is scaring me. So, why do You care?'

'Well, my child,' He said, to me, 'I care about everyone that I meet.
For I have this problem, that I believe everyone needs some love.
And there are those that do not know, or never have had the chance to feel
This thing called love, that's sent to us on the wings of a dove.'

'It's pure and simple and flies around, spreading lightness wherever it goes.
It touches your heart, with its tenderness and flutters, silently, inside.'
I'd never seen a dove before, this love thing sounded very weird.
It felt very strange to be sitting here, I wanted to go run and hide.

But, hadn't I just done that and found somewhere very different.
And the longer I stayed, the more it seemed not to frighten me, anymore.
I might as well find out about this love thing, not that I am here.
For I've nowhere else to go, right now, and my feet are very sore!

'So, please, can You explain to me and show me more of this 'love'?'
I start to get excited, for this is all so new and I feel safe upon His knee.
I'm sure glad that I got lost and found my way to this very place.
For, I think, I'll never leave, this 'love' thing, sounds so good to me.

42

My Clumsiness

You talk to me
In the most peculiar ways
And it's always
When I'm having—one of those days.
When I feel
Like I've got two left feet
And I drop
My food when I try to eat.
I put my shirt
On backwards—sometimes, inside out!
I even go to drive
The wrong way round a roundabout!
I'm just not myself.
I'm in a pickle.
I'm uncoordinated,
My mind is being fickle.
It's full of nonsense,
Heading in different directions.
It's no wonder,
That I am touched by these afflictions!
So, You bring me back to earth,
With a bump.
Try to startle me
So that my mind cannot jump
Around in circles,
Getting nowhere, very fast.
It is reminded to stop,

To take note, at last.
So that I can relax
And remind me to be present.
So I think
When I am clumsy—it was Heaven sent!

43

Don't Worry

Please God, don't do this to me right now
For I have enough things on my plate.
The last thing I need is to get some more
Of these things, that I really do hate.
To be constantly worrying that I cannot
Live in some sort of comfort,
Is starting to make me wonder if you have
Devised a brand new plot,
To test me, yet again, and make sure
That I'll follow You, regardless
Of whether I am rich or poor, because
At the moment I am penniless.
I'm just about down to my last cent,
I haven't got a brass razzoo.
So, if I go and get a speeding fine,
Should I send the bill to You?
For I was miles away, on a different planet,
When I just plain forgot
To check on the speed that I was doing,
So I think this is really funny—not!!
That I was trying to make some time
To spend with You tonight,
And just when I was nearly home,
The multinova caught me in its sight.
So, here I sit and wonder—why
Is this all happening to me?
For I would like, one day, to live
Without worrying and be free
To spend some time enjoying the things,
That I'd really like to do.

To laugh, to run, to play and have fun,
And do all these things—with You,
Not worry if I'm going to have enough
To pay for all the basic things,
Let alone be faced with something else
That the postman brings.
So, please God, I'm asking You, if there
Is any way You can intervene,
And check to see—if there was a fault
With the multnova machine.
Because, I did not think that I was
Driving way too fast, instead,
I was preoccupied, with the
Thoughts, that were going around inside my head,
That were trying to save me time,
So that I could spend more of it with You.
So, please God, can You help me to take care,
When I'm on the road—can You?

44

Looking for You

I had a dream, that I was wandering in the dark, trying to return
something that I had found.
I wandered up and down the streets, and, all of this was very familiar ground.
And then I saw a door that I thought I recognized. So, I went to see if it
was open.
I pushed it gently and had a look inside, to see if this is for what I was looking.

I stepped in and walked around for a while, for there was so much space
in there.
It was so quite and rather eerie, but, I felt at home with the peaceful feel
in the air.
In the silence I heard a voice, saying "I'm over here, would you like some
nice hot tea?"
'Oh, yes please, and, if I can, have You got some muffins? For I'm feeling
rather hungry.'

I sat down quietly, while I waited for You to bring all these things to
where I sat.
Patiently, I looked around, it all seemed so familiar that I asked. 'Where I
was at?'
Sitting down, beside me, as He place my food on the table He said that.
'I was safely home.'
With a puzzled look upon my face, I asked Him. 'If His head was filled
with crazy foam?'

'No, my child, I've been waiting here, for a very long time. To serve and
give you all your heart desires.
You've sampled lots of others wares, and were not satisfied. For you, they
were false mentors, cheats and liars.

You used to come here as a child, taking your time to choose the candy
that you really liked to eat.
So, if you look over there, you will see the shelves, full of yummy things,
that are so sweet.'

'Oh, my goodness, I remember now.' I jump up excited and run over to
where I see
Everything in the world that I love, but the grown ups said were so 'bad
for me'.
'Can I please have some now, for I've missed all this.' Like a child, I plead.
'Help yourself, I'm always here, the shelves are always full of everything
that you need.'

They taste so good, I fall in love, with their sweetness, again. My heart is
full of joy.
For I've found what I was trying to return, it was me. I found my child.
'Oh boy!'
I turn around and thank Him. For now, I understand that He waited,
patiently, for me to return.
For me to find the sweetness and love, that my child held the candle,
waiting for me to burn.

To light the dark nights and keep me warm and loved,
When I thought I was so alone.
When really You were waiting here, for me to walk through the door
And call Your home, my own.

45

Roses in the Park

Life is beautiful. It's a bed of roses.
But, Jesus Christ and Holy Moses!
How did You know? What did You see?
When You decided, to put Your faith in me.

You planted the seed, then let it rest.
Your time, in me, You did invest.
You kept me waiting, in the dark.
Strengthening my roots, in life's park.

You watched me break out of the ground.
And gently nurtured any flaws You found.
You sat and watched me, from afar.
By day, sending Your sun. At night, a star.

The seasons, they come. The seasons, they go.
You showered me with love and watched me grow.
And even when it was cold outside
You were always there, right by my side.

To grow up strong, You gave to me
A pile of shit, through which, I could not see.
You protected me, when I was weak
And seemed to be stuck in the mud, so to speak.

You had the faith, that I would learn.
Knowing, that in the end, to You, I would turn
And ask You, if You'd like to help me
Wipe the mud, from my eyes, so that I could see.

You pruned my stem and then my branches.
And, in Your wisdom, You took no chances.
And then You, tenderly, whispered in my ear.
'You can open your eyes now, have no fear.

For it's time to wake up, now, it is spring.
It's time to look, at your beauty, within.
You have grown so beautiful, that's for sure.
A rose made in Heaven, that is so pure.'

46

God's Little House

There is a place I go to, when I want some peace.
It's always there, waiting, for me to come back to
When I need some time to be, or just to hang out.
It is a place we all know well. Every house has a loo!

I go in there and lock the door, sit down and relax.
I read a book, or, just vacantly stare into space.
I look at the cracks in the walls, maintenance, I'll have to do.
Then, there's always the ants on the floor, having the usual race!

As I sit and ponder, I feel safe inside these walls.
For they are close enough to touch, I could be in a cocoon.
Hey, maybe, I'm a caterpillar, who is sleeping on the job.
Or, maybe, I'm a spider, and this is the web, that I'll finish soon.

I laugh cos it's funny, the thoughts that go through my head.
When I'm sitting in my silence, sometimes the thoughts make me blush.
But, I need to concentrate on the job, of why I came in here.
Cos, when I walked through the door, I was in such a rush.

Now, I remember, I was pissed off and a little shitty too.
I'd had some problems during the day, that I'd held on to.
So, I'd come to talk to You, in Your little house.
Cos, You are my friend and these things, I'd like to share with You.

You listen very patiently, while I spill them out.
Accepting all I have to say, with Your arms open wide
As I wipe away my tears, You silently forgive me
Then You flush away my fears, so I no longer have to hide.

I thank You for Your patience, whilst putting up with me.
For I'll come back and visit soon—we talk every day.
I would not miss, for anything, the conversations that we have.
I love the way You make me feel. You take my troubles away.

47

Albert Edward

Albert Edward came to me. He asked if I'd like to see.
As I blindly stumbled round, he held my hand, for me, he'd found.

'I'm Albert Edward, how do you do? I think you've just stepped in poo!
Can I be of some assistance?' He asked, with some persistence.

Stubbornly, I stamped my foot. Feeling silly, cos I'd put
Myself in such a big mess. I'd even got some on my dress!

He offered me his handkerchief. My thank you, was very brief.
Turning, smiling, gently at me. 'It's my pleasure,' softly, said he.

He held my hand, as I stood, barefoot, cleaning what I could.
Very quietly, saying to me. 'I think it's clean now. Can you see?'

Standing back, I had a look. Then I went and dropped my book.
'It was my favourite.' I cried out. 'We'll find another, have no doubt.'

Holding my hand, he took me around the corner, then we did see
A new store. It was a delight. Oh, so new and shiny bright!

It felt so strange and so new. He said, softly. 'Choose a few.
Take your time, stay awhile.' As he walked me down the aisle.

I cried out, totally awestruck. 'Why did you help me out of the muck.
You are so fine, I am so messy. I wear rags, and you are dressy.'

Smiling, he looked down at me. 'You are a child, come and see
The love inside, that we can share. Rich or poor, it's all there.

We only have to open the door, look inside and find there's more
Love and goodness, for every one. Here's some for you, my little one.'

So, Albert Edward, I thank you, for helping me, to clean my shoe.
For your love and persistence, and guiding me, from a distance.

I know that we will meet again So, please hold me, until then,
In your loving arms. I pray, you'll keep me safe, until that day.

48

My Gift from God

I thank You for this special gift
That You have just for me.
I know that I did not find it
Under the Christmas tree.
The Easter Bunny did not hide it
In her Easter basket.
The Halloween witches, never
Locked it in a casket.
I know You kept it in Your heart,
Til I came to You.
And asked You, very humbly,
If there was anything I could do,
Cos I'd handed all my troubles over,
Now my mind was free.
I was just sort of wondering
If You had a job for me?
So, thank You, once again, dear God
For saving this one for me
Cos I think it's rather special
That you set my heart free
To listen very carefully
To everything You say.
To feel Your love and share with You,
Every single day,
The beauty that surrounds us—
That others sometimes miss.
So, I send to You my thank you God,

Sealed with love, a hug and a kiss,
And promise that I will share
Your love, that is forever true,
With everyone who wants to see
The gift, that's inside, from You.

49

My Best Friend

Never judge a book by its cover, they used to say to me.
We should all love one another, for in this world we are free.
But, I grew up and soon would discover
That when some people say one thing, they mean another.

It was so confusing, I did not know which way to turn.
Not knowing whom to trust, or anything that I learn.
What is true for me, or what could be a lie.
Between my ego and my self, we did not see eye to eye.

My self, I decided to have a rest, to go on a long holiday,
For I got very tired of all this confusion, every single day.
I packed my bags and went away, as far as I could go.
Then, half way up Mount Everest, I got lost in the snow.

I called for You to help me out, I didn't know what to do,
For I was frozen to my core and was starting to turn blue.
You took my hand and led me, for I was blinded by the light,
Out of the snow, where I'd been lost, for it was brilliant white.

My pride, at first, did not like the fact that I had returned.
It tried to trip me up a lot, questioning everything I had learned.
It burnt my face in the sun, when I was thawing out.
It threw away my directory, and tried to choose a different route.

It even tried to stop my thoughts, as I write this down.
There are some times that, I believe, he could live in another town.
But, that would be to run away again and not stand face to face,
And stare at him in the eyes, as he tried to play his ace.

For now that I have warmed my heart and found You are inside,
I no longer have to run from him and think that You had lied
About the fact that we are all free and born of one true love,
That You have all of the answers and You watch us from above

So, to myself, I say that I will always trust in what I feel.
And read the book You have given me, for within, its love is real.
For You have written every word and You always say what You mean.
You did not judge. You set me free. You're the best friend I've ever seen.

50

Housework

Come on now, tidy up your house.
Get it in order, be a good little mouse.
Pull up the rug, sweep under there.
Please remember to pull out the chair.

The mess is not going to go away,
So, why not get busy and deal with it today.
You can try and put it off,
But, all that dust will make you cough.

It you want some help, then just ask
And I will help you, to complete your task.
I have some tools, that you might need.
They've got instructions, that you can read.

They may seem hard to understand,
But, if you'd like, I can give you a hand.
Because two sets of hands are better than one,
It won't be long, before the work is done.

It will be quite easy, once you try.
And we'll get quite mucky, I tell no lie!
But, we can bathe at the end of the day,
Knowing that we found the way.

To work together and discover,
That we both need one another
To clean up the mess and sort it out.
To find the way, there is no doubt.

And it takes a lot of looking under,
In the corners, and no wonder!
If we store it all away,
And say we'll deal with it another day

The task, at hand, may overwhelm us
And, wanting not to make a big fuss,
We would close our eyes and shut the door.
Then, we would not see it, anymore!

And even though we would choose not to care.
All of the mess, it would still be there!
All stored up and hidden away.
Waiting for us, to face, on another day.

51

Bear and Mouse

Two grown people living in a house.
One called Big bear, the other called Mouse

'I'm big and strong, look what I can do.'

'I'm small and sweet, I'll be there for you.'

Bear plods around and works hard all day.
He gives himself no time to play.

Mouse scurries around, all day long.
She has no time to sing a song

Bear got grumpy. 'My back is sore.'

Mouse got dizzy, scurrying around the floor.

They asked for help. Was it too late?
'Just take a rest, sit down and wait.'

One day Bear heard such a din.
Excited, Mouse said. 'Let's join in.'

Off they went, a little scared.
And together, both their souls, they bared.

They found a love, that is pure and true.
And, together said. 'I'd like to share it with you.'

Now, they both grow, strong and free.

Bear and Mouse

Found

God's House

You see!

52

Mighty Mouse

Mouse has been doing exercises,
To help make her fit and strong.
For she was so little, others did not see her,
So she was always getting trodden on.

She went on a holiday,
With her best friend—who was Bear.
Together, they decided,
To help each other find a strength to share.

So, hand in hand, they took
One step at a time. Slowly moving forward.
Helping each other, in their own peculiar ways,
So each other understood

The strengths, the weaknesses,
The times to rest, before taking the next step.
To compromise, to stand strong,
They both became quite adept

At listening to each other,
Being aware of each others needs and wants.
Yet, patiently, accepting their differences.
Instead of being frustrated by do's and don'ts.

So, now they support each other,
On their journey down life's winding road.
Meeting lots of friends along the way,
Including rabbit, tiger and toad.

Their journey is eventful,
With lots of fun and adventures along the way.
Together, they are thankful that,
They decided to help each other that fateful day.

For, since then, their lives have been turned upside down,
Filled with a brand new vitality.
Mouse found her inner strength, its radiance so bright,
That everyone, her spirit, can now see.

53

Tending the Flock

You are my shepherd, who is herding My sheep
Into the fold, for Me to keep.
They play in the meadow and have lots of fun.
For here, there is no need to run.
They frolic around and are completely unaware
That I am here, and you are there.

They happily eat the fresh green grass
And skip amongst the flowers.
When they get tired, they lay down to rest,
And sleep for hours and hours.

Strange sounds awaken them from their sleep.
They venture, slowly, and take a peep.
There is someone here, to join in their fun.
Lets play a game, see how far we can run.
They frolic around and play—catch me, if you dare.
For I am here, and you are there.

They feel so free, they leap about
Having so much fun.
'This feels like Heaven, it must be love.
Have I had too much sun?'

Trust what you feel. You're no longer asleep.
Welcome home my little sheep.
I'll show you everything, it is such fun.
Stay and play with Me, in the sun.
You can frolic around, My home with you, I share.
For you are here, and I am there.

54

Bugs and Flu's

Hugs are infectious, you can catch them
Like the flu!
There is plenty for everyone,
Even for me and for you.
Small ones, big ones,
They are a lot like bugs!
For it is very surprising
Who can give the very best hugs.

Straight from the heart,
They zap you, get under your skin.
Fooling you by their appearance,
Normally, you would never let them in.
So, take a chance and give a hug.
Open up your arms and try it.
Let the warmth flow out of your heart,
Just a little bit.

You'll be surprised at the effect.
For, as you give, you receive so much more.
The greatest pleasure, the feeling inside,
You've opened up the store.
Of love, unconditional,
It's far more toxic than the flu.
Yet, it's such a friendly bug,
To share between me and you.

So, why are we scared
Of catching it?
There is really nothing

To fear.
For, life is really
Quite beautiful.
When
You hold your loved ones near.

IN SICKNESS

55

Amazing

I am so amazed at everything I see
At all the things in life, that You are showing me.

I always knew that I loved You. Now I know for sure
That You are always with me. I wasn't sure before.

I was blind and walking around, in a bit of a daze.
I just couldn't find my way through the maze

Of all the things, that try to disguise themselves
Pretending they lead to You, that we can discover ourselves.

Now, I know for sure, that You are the only One
That shows me everything that will ever be done.

Your love is in my heart. Your light is in my eyes.
You are always in my head. You bring me down to size.

For, when I do not listen to You, You gently knock my head.
You make me lie down quietly, snuggle up with You in bed.

And listen to Your gentle voice, that softly says to me.
'Listen quietly to your heart, for it will set you free

To open up and be all things, that are here, waiting for you.
For while you were lost in the maze, My love, inside you, grew.

So, take some love and kindness, that's there inside your heart.
Take a step outside the maze, and your journey will start.'

56

Skin Deep

They say that beauty is only skin deep
But, it I take off my mask, I may fall in a heap.

I went away from You, and slid from grace.
For there was too much pain, for me to face.

So, I put on a mask and there it stays
To live in this world and cope with its ways.

I'd like to take off the mask and throw it away.
For I'd like to come out and play today.

But, it feels so tight and it covers my face.
And, how can I see? I may trip over my lace.

It's spoiling my fun, I'd like it to go.
If you know how to help, please, let me know.

What I may find, may not be very pretty.
But, to keep it in place, it makes me feel shitty.

It has got too small and I'm starting to break out.
It has got to go, that, I have no doubt.

It may be scary, what I have to face, out there.
But, to be free of the pain, my face, I have to bare.

I pulled the mask away. God, it was so sore!
Now, I'm feeling so exposed. It is so raw.

Please, do you know, if there is somewhere I can go
To bathe my face, to help heal the wounds that show?

'Come, sit with me awhile. I'll wash your sores away.
Lay down and gently rest your head. It's safe for you to stay.'

It took some time to heal. But, now the world I face.
I asked if I could return to You, and You showed me grace.

I can see clearly now, that, if I ever fall.
You will pick me up. You will always answer my call.

You will hold my hand, while I face my fear.
You love and protect me. You will always be near.

57

Please Hold Me

I need someone to hold me. I'm feeling so hurt.
I think I fell over, into the dirt.
'Do you have some time, to give me a hug?
Please sit down, with me, on the rug.'

I'm feeling very hurt. I'm shaking all over.
I'm feeling very cold. I need another pullover.
'Can you please, just hold me tight
And tell me, that it's going to be alright.'

My head is pounding. I'm so confused.
All over my body, I'm feeling bruised.
'Please, can you gently stroke my hair?
Cos it hurts me, if you touch me there.

Why is it that I'm feeling this way?'
I hear myself, very quietly say.

'Can You hold me closely.' I start to weep.
'And wrap Your arms around me while I sleep.
Will You protect me, through this dark night
And tell me that it's going to be alright?

So, if I wake, will You still be there,
Holding me gently, with tender loving care?
Will You wipe away the tears, from my eyes,
Cross Your heart and promise to tell me no lies

About the pain I must face, for my wounds to heal?
And, help me see, that the hurt that I feel
Will fade slowly away, in to the past.
And, no longer, its dark shadow, will it cast.

So, please hold me close, but, don't turn out the light.
Cos, with Your help, I think it will be alright.

58

Waiting for You to Reply

There is something
I just have to say.
And, your opinion
I'm not trying to sway.
I know this might sound
Rather weird.
Maybe, the strangest thing
You've ever heard!
But, I think,
I may know a place
If you'd like to go
And try and face
The problem with
The pain in your back.
If you have the faith,
I think, it's the right track.

I know your pain
I've been there too.
I'm trying to find the help
That's true, for you.
So, if you'd like
To take a chance
Be free of pain.
Be free to dance.
If you would like to keep
An open heart.
I'll show you a way,
That you can start.
And, if you believe,

You will have a life
Supported and strong,
Free of strife.

I'm answering your call,
Now, it's up to you.
To keep an open mind.
Place some trust in Me too.
To open up
And, face all those fears
That you hid from others,
For years and years.
I'll be by your side,
Every step of the way.
For, I've waited a lifetime,
For this very day.

59

Hiding Our Troubles Away

If you keep all your troubles in you, they fester, down inside.
For really, they have nowhere else to go. There's nowhere else to hide!
They find themselves little pockets, there are plenty inside of you.
Lots of little secret pockets, that are hidden from your view.

But, just the same as our overcoat, if we try to put too much in,
Eventually it all falls out, or a hole appears—from within!
The mess then spills out, internally, and goes to places we can't see.
It creeps around, inside us, because it is trying to set itself free
From the pain of hiding in those pockets—for so very long.
For we had put it in some places, where it really did not belong.

We had hidden all our love from You, way down deep inside our heart.
Now, that had seemed, in this world, a very good place to start.

Whenever we would get angry, we put it in a pocket, called our liver.
But, that pocket can get really full and then it will all spill over.

In to our gut, where it adds to all the fear we keep down there.

And all the sadness we do not wish to face, is hidden by our hair.

We try to hold on to these things, but, it gets to be a pain in the neck.

And the weight we carry round inside, spills out in to our back.

We cannot run away from it all, because our legs can't carry us.

For they buckle under the strain, as we try not to make a fuss
Of all the troubles that we keep inside. So, instead of sending them south,
Why don't we just open up, dig deep inside and throw them out of our mouth?

Then, we can be free of our troubles, and make a brand new start.

And find, each day, the love for You, that we hide inside our heart.

60

Intuition

I have a sore head and
It won't go away.
What did I do
To deserve this today?
For it's slowly got worse,
As the day has progressed.
Could it be
That I'm feeling a bit stressed?
I did not think that
There was anything worrying me.
But, my head
Was thumping and pressuring me.
It only decided to listen
And go away
When a friend rang me to say
'Good day .'
For I had asked it.
'Why was it there?'
Had there been something that I
Had to share?
As soon as she called
I then realized
The reason my head hurt
Was in front of my eyes.
For my intuition had been trying
To tell me
That she was going to call and
'Would I be free?'
For she once got knocked out
By a ball

And she had trouble remembering
Anything at all!
I had been thinking of her
Earlier that day
So, maybe, it was a reminder, to me,
In a way.
For when I did not listen and remember
To call
That You'd find another way
To show me, that all
Of the ways in which You try
To teach us.
If one does not work
Then, another will reach us.

61

Hocus Pocus

You need a clear mind, if you wand to focus.
I used to think—that was hocus pocus!

Until everything that I tried to do
Was just too much, for me, to get through.
Try as I might, I could not think
It was there in my mind, right on the brink.
'Dam and blast, it's all a kerfuddle.
Oh my God, I'm in such a muddle!.

My mouth says 'yes', my brain says 'no'.
I'm upside down, don't know which way to go.
I went to the doctor. The pills didn't work.
Then I fell over. I felt such a jerk!
Sat on my arse, with a broken ankle.
The mess in my head, started to rankle.

I had some time to sit around.
To clear my mind, it was not sound.
There was a battle, with the crap in my head.
The shit went flying—it had to be said.
It got cleaned up, at the end of the day.
But, it was not pretty—I have to say.

It cleared my mind, so that I could focus.
Now, I know—it's not hocus pocus.

62

Emptiness

I have this hunger, I don't know why.
I cannot fill it, no matter how I try.
I hold out a bowl for you to help me fill.
It sits there waiting. It's empty, still.

I have nice clothes and lots of shoes.
And people tell me, 'you've got the baby blues'!
I hold out my hand for them to hold.
They turn away. They crumble and fold.

I get in the car and try to escape.
You take the wheel and enfold me in Your cape.
I ask for help, but they're still asleep.
So, I silently, fall in a heap.

I put up my shield, I feel so numb.
I'll prove to them I'm not so dumb.
I go to college, and get a new house.
But, inside, I'm still a scared little mouse.

You gently wake me, with Your soft ugg boot.
But, I stay asleep, behind a drink or a root.
The pain hurts so much. Please, take it away.
I'm on my knees, God, please help me today.

You hold me gently in Your arms.
As, slowly, my defenses You disarm.
And, as I slowly face my fears,
You tenderly wipe away my tears.

It gets too hard. I try to run.
There's too much pain. There is no fun.
I fall down and I lay there—broken.
I did not realize, that, You had spoken.

You hold me gently, while I rest.
Cocooned in Your love, I was Your guest.
You taught me to crawl, before I could walk.
You taught me to listen and hear You talk.

So, now Your love fills up my bowl
I realize, that I was a lost soul.
I surrender to You—with all my heart.
Knowing that Your love—will never depart.

63

Friends Like You

I have some friends, they are the best you can have.
They even hold you up—as you spew down the lav!
They'll have a drink, or two, with you.
Then they'll hold you up, as you spew down the loo!
They are always there when my sorrows I drown.
We have another drink, there's no need to feel down.
But, where are they when I want to face this feeling
And, I'm getting so sick of sending myself reeling
All over the place, as I get drunk and fall over?
Where are they now that I have found a new lover?

'Come on out tonight with us, for we're going to party on.'
Is what they say to me, when I say what I have done.
But, when I let them know that I would prefer to stay at home,
They all think that I've gone nuts, and wonder 'what went wrong?'
I try to explain that drinking makes me sick—and I choose not to.
I'd rather sit and talk with You, instead of spewing down the loo.
'Who is this person that's stolen your heart? You have really changed.
Come on, get out and party on, it's already been arranged.'
I decline their offer, knowing, that they think I'm rejecting them.
But, I know the friend I have found, is more than a bit of a gem.

He loves me, no matter what I do. He wants, for me, only the best.
He holds my hand and hugs me, whether I'm busy, or when I rest.
He listens to my sorrows. He's there, sharing in all my joy.
He never puts me down, at all. But, nudges me when I get coy.
I might not talk to Him for a while, but, He still waits for me.

He's the best friend I could ever have, but, they still choose not to see.
For they are jealous of the fact, that I found Your love.
They do not seem to understand at all, for me, You are above
Anything that I could ever find—down a toilet bowl.
For Your love found a way—deep down inside my soul.

You crept in slowly and then introduced Yourself to me.
You gained my trust, by being You and letting me see
That all around me was Your love, I only had to ask.
For You would always be there for me. It was a pleasant task
For You to hold my hand, hug me tight, or softly kiss my cheek.
To keep me warm in Your embrace, when I was feeling weak.
You walk with me. We have lots of fun. You have a great sense of humour.
And, when I want my silent space, You do not start a rumour
That I have lost my love for You, because, You know for sure
That I would never walk away again—from a love that is pure.

You are my best friend in the whole wide world, and, I love You so.
I love You truly, yes I do. But, I think You already know.

64

Aching for You

I woke up this morning with an ache, somewhere inside.
I could not seem to find it. It was trying to hide.
I thought I had a tummy ache and needed to go to the loo.
But, no, I discovered it was not that. Maybe, I had the flu!

For this ache seemed to be spreading all around inside.
It was getting harder and harder to find a place to hide..
I went back to bed, maybe, I just needed to get some more sleep!
For it could be that I was tired, with the busy life that I keep.
But, I could not rest, for it hurt to even lay on my side.
I was aching all over. It was no longer bothering to hide.

What on earth could I do, to make this ache just go away?
As I lay there in my bed, to You, I started to pray.
'Please God, help me, for I know not what to do.'
All I know, for sure, is that I really have not got the flu.

Because, not matter what I do, this aching feeling I cannot shake.
It's only when I call to You, that I realize that this ache
Is my body trying to tell me that I need to talk to You.
That You are aching to hear from me, so, You start with a visit to the loo.
If that does not work, then, with the flu, You lay me down to rest.
I really must take my hat off to You, You really try Your best.

You know all the places, that, I go to try and hide.
But, You still stay with me, slowly, tearing down my walls inside.
Until I go back to the place where this ache truly did start.
Back to when You created me and stepped inside my heart.

For You are there, always, and have been since the day I was born.
You just remind me of Your presence, when I feel my heart is torn.
For the day that I took my first breathe, here on this earth
I was torn apart from You. My heart's been aching—since birth.
So, when I feel an ache again I'll stop first and look inside.
Into my heart and talk to You—I won't run and hide.

65

Face Mask

Why is it, that, I do not want to see?
My face—is aching and it's hurting me.
My eyes—are itching. I want to scratch them out.
It irritates to open them and look all about.
My jaw—just wants to be left alone.
As it feels like it's been chewing a bone!
Inside my ears—I have an itch I can't scratch.
They're both burning hot—at least they match!
My nose—it tickles and wants to sneeze.
Is it the pollen, that was brought by the breeze?
My mouth—is dry and has a funny taste.
Maybe, I spoke with too much haste!
My cheeks—are flushed and tingling too.
Was it the wine? For I've had a few!
Even my hair—has got in on the act.
Maybe, with my face, it made a pact!

Because my head and everything on it
Feels like it is falling apart—bit by bit,
And has decided that it's had enough,
It would like to get rid of the rest of the stuff.
'So please hurry up. I haven't got all day.'
To the state of my head, is what I say.
'I'd like you to take off the rest of the mask,
So that I can see the beginning of my task.
I would appreciate, that, it will happen soon.
I have no preference—night or noon.'

So, I'm asking You, to help me see my truth,
And let go of this mask—'it's irritating, strewth!!'
So, until then, my face, I will try not to touch.
But, I'll look inside, hopefully, it won't be too much
For me to face, for I know You are by my side.
And, when the mask comes off, I'll no longer hide
Myself from You. For, I'll be free to see
All the love, that You, have been keeping for me.

66

Gods Cure for Headaches

The pain in my head won't go away. It's making me sick. It started today.
It's thumping so loud, it wants to get out. It hurts so much. I want to
scream and shout!
No matter which way I turn my head, I wish that I could just go to bed
And sleep all night. So, that when I wake, the pain in my head would no
longer make
Me wish, that I could just take off my head—and put it somewhere else instead.
Panadol—just does not seem to work. I throw it up. I feel such a jerk!
For it's everywhere. I've made such a mess! How can I clear it up? Just let
me guess!
I hold my nose—because it stinks—and, get on my knees, with a cloth in
my hand.
I clean most of it up, then I sit down. Put on my pyjamas and dressing gown.
I curl up on my favourite chair. My head's still thumping. It's not fair!
The men, with their hammers, won't go away. 'Please God, do something,
I don't want them to stay.'

I close my eyes and look inside my head—at all those me, that I wished
were dead!
Each one is trying to hammer into me—all of their pain, that they don't
wish to see.
'Put your hammers down.' I ask them. 'Please.' For my pain, I wish to ease.
'For, if you have no wish to see, then, please don't take your pain out on me.
I have enough of my own.' I politely said. 'So, please, take your pain and
get out of my head.
It hurts me too much, to look after yours too. So, please, just take it back
home with you.'
I start to cry, it's just all too much. My head hurts—ever so much.
'God, please, just take this pain away. I no longer need it, anyway.'
My head feels like it's going to explode. At least then, I will be rid of this load!

As I doze, I start to dream that I'm floating—in a stream
That is 'oh so warm' and as it covers my head—washes away those men
that I want dead.
They sink to the bottom of the stream. Weighted down by their
hammers—in my dream.
My head feels so light. It feels so free—of the men, with their hammers,
that tortured me.
As I float, I look around and see a beautiful tree, that appears to be
Holding out its branches, for me to reach. I stretch out my arms and take
one in each.
It pulls me out. It is so strong. It cradles me close and starts to sing me a song.
I feel so safe and secure. As I lay and listen to the words of the
song—they say—

'Just let me hold you close, in My arms. I will protect you and keep you
safe from harm.
I'll love you tenderly and watch you grow. Pain, from Me, you will never
know.
For, in My heart, I carry the seeds of all things good, of all your needs.
And, if you ever fall away from Me, my tears will keep you safe. You will see.
For they wash away all of your fears and leave you free to live your years
In love and peace, with Me by your side. Free from pain, that, you won't
have to hide.'

As I drifted, in and out of sleep, these words in my head, I did keep.
And, when I awoke, at the break of day, the pain in my head—had
gone away!
I was still curled up on my favourite chair. Wrapped in Your arms, so glad
You were there,
To sing to me and let me know that Your love, You will always show
To me, when, in my pain I cannot see that You are always
here—inside—with me.

67

Praying to God

When I get sick I get so grumpy

My bed is cold and my pillow is lumpy!

My head hurts and I feel so ill

I go to the doctors and get a pill

I go back to bed and fall asleep

Then, out of bed, I have to leap.

And try and make it to the loo.

For, I need to pray to You.

I ask God, to 'help me, please.'

'Oh, there's the pizza, it had cheese!'

I feel better, now it's out.

But, my head still hurts. 'Please don't shout.'

Off to bed, again, I go.

Tossing and turning, to and fro.

When, at last, I fall asleep

Lovingly, my soul, You keep.

68

Sick and Tired

Why am I so sick and tired?
I feel like my circuits need to be rewired.

I cough and sneeze. I have no energy.
What the hell is wrong with me?

I eat, I sleep, I enjoy my work.
My responsibilities, I try not to shirk.

Yet, all the while, I continue to be
Sick and tired. What is wrong with me?

My motivation is disappearing—fast!
I could not care if I came first or last.

All of the wind has blown out of my sails.
I've no fight left. Please, tell me, what ails?

For I'm sick and tired of feeling like this.
All I want in my life—is a little bliss.

A small piece of time, that I call my own.
Where I could sit still and be shown.

A place to go to when I'm sick and tired.
'Oh, my God!' You've given me what I required.

I did not see it, for, I was so tired, so sick.
And, now I realized that it was no trick.

You tried to reach me—to rest my soul.
In the end I got sick—so that I could become whole!

69

A New Trick

My stomach is churning, around and around.
And, it is starting to make me feel sick.
I did not know that it knew how
To do this wonderful new trick!
It feels just like a washing machine,
Tumbling everything around inside.
I wish I could open it up and
See if anything is knotted or tied.
For, it feels like something is stuck
And cannot find its way out.
And, it's starting to clog everything up,
Sending everything around and about.
Why is it doing this thing to me?
I really, really would like to know.
Where did it learn this new trick?
Is there a new magic show?
For, I'd like to know how it did it
So that I can solve the puzzle
Of why my stomach is tied up in knots
And feels all in a kerfuffle!
For, it's making lots of strange noises,
Like something is trying to get out.
It feels like it is going to explode—
Of that, I have no doubt.
And, where will everything go to then,
When it can no longer trick me?
For, there are only a choice of two places—
That I am able to see.
It can either come up into the open—
Where I can see where it got tied.

Or, it can disappear—into a bottomless pit—
Where it smells like something has died!
For, this new trick, that my stomach has,
Just cannot make things disappear.
It only tries to fool me into believing
If I can't see it—I will not hear.
But, I can still feel things moving around—
If I sit still long enough.
So, stomach, if you are listening to me.
You can play tricks—but, you are not that tough!

70

I've Had Enough!

I have this pressure in my head and it is really bugging me.
I wish I could take the top off, and, set the pressure free!

For, it's holding all my feelings in, and, they'd really like to escape.
They keep banging on the inside, and, I'm sure they are altering the shape
Of my head, for, my nose is getting bigger, and, my ears are sticking out.
Something keeps leaking out of my eyes, and, 'I'm losing my hair' I shout.

And, I'm getting quite bad tempered, as it is giving me a headache.
I want to know if there is anything I can do—to stop this stupid ache?

I bang and crash around the place, or, that is how it seems.
For, the noise inside my head—makes whispers sound like screams!

I wish I knew, just what it was, that is doing all these things to me.
Maybe, all these feelings are arguing amongst themselves and cannot see
That I would really like to sit down and take the pressure away,
Or my head is going to explode and I cannot cope with anymore mess today!

'I've had enough of this noise.' I say to the feelings inside of my head.

'So, you can all sort yourselves out and quiet down—or you're gonna be dead!

I know you all have your problems, but, it's time to sort them all out,

Instead of piling them up inside my head, because, there's no spare room
to move about!

So, I'm taking charge now. There's going to be some changes made
around here!'

I think I'll have a heart to heart with my feelings, and, show them there's
nothing to fear.
Then they'll know that it is quite safe. There's no need to escape from me.
And, instead of giving me a headache, maybe, learn to love and just be
Who they are—instead of fighting amongst themselves. For there are no
winners or losers.

There is just love and acceptance, of all their differences, and, no need to
blow their fuses!

71

Leaving It All Up To You

Today
I have decided, to leave it all up to You
For, every time
I do it my way, I end up in the poo!
I end up
Running around in circles and getting nowhere—fast!
I end up
Racing around a lot and always coming last.
So, I've decided,
That, from now on, I'm going to take it easy.
And, let You
Do all the work, so, I won't get out of breath and wheezy!
I'm going to
Sit back and enjoy life—for a little while.
I'm going to
Do all the things I like—the ones that make me smile.
I do hope
That You do not mind—that I'm leaving it all up to You.
In fact, I think
You'd prefer it that way, for then, it will be easier to
Get the job done
That is waiting—which is to talk to me.
But
All the time that I run around, I never get the chance to see.
That You
Are waiting silently—trying to get a message through.
That there is
Something important, that, You want me to do!

72

Locked in the Loo!

It's funny
How the brain, seems to fly out of the window.
Whenever
We get sick or tired and, at the time, we don't know how
We got ourselves
Into this mess, and, we have no idea what to do.
So
We just give up, at last! And, throw the question out to You.

'Please God, help me.'
For I 'm feeling very sick, and, I want to die.

"What on earth, can I do?'
To stop this aching in my body, I cry.

Where
Does my ego go, when my body is crying out in pain?
It seems, to me,
That he is nowhere to be found—when I'm going insane!
With
This torture, that I feel, when my body is complaining to me
That
It has had enough of the way in which I live, and, it's time to see
What
Life is all about. Instead of thinking 'I have to suffer to be me!'
Instead
Of knowing, that, there is joy and love and we are meant to be free.

So
What happens to my ego? Is he feeling sick and tired too?
Or did You
Play a trick on him and decide to lock him in the loo
So You
Could spend some time, with me, and generally get straight to the point
And ask me
If I am going to live my life, or keep these aches in my joints?

73

Letting My Troubles Go

I have a lump in my throat—it gets in the way. My eyes keep watering. 'It irritates me!' I say.
I've got the snuffles. 'Can you please pass the tissues.' I yawn my head off. I'm so tired—it's an issue!
That, I would just like to crawl into bed, cos, I think I've got a cold, in my head.
My throat is sore—I don't feel like talking. But, I know that I have to keep on walking
Down the road and around the corner. I'm not going to be able to slip under the bed cover.

For, first, there is something that I have to do. I had already started it—before I got this flu.
I was on my way to see You—I have no doubt. For, there was something, that, I just had to find out.
Could it be true, the things that I had heard? I had to know. But, my eyes water, my vision is blurred.
My head is thumping and I'm going to sneeze. My chest feel heavy, now, it starts to wheeze.
I won't give up, because, I'm nearly there. Just around the corner. 'God, help me!' I swear.
I'm feeling very sick and now I wish I'd gone to bed. My nose is running. I've got cotton wool in my head!

But, it's too late now, because—there—You wait. Not surprised to see me—in this terrible state.
You comfort me and sit me right down. Let me pour out my troubles. You, do not frown.
But, sit there waiting, patiently, for me to finish. Passing me the tissues. Now, I'm feeling rather sheepish!

For, I'm feeling much better—now I've talked to You. So, maybe, I
haven't got a cold, or the flu!

Maybe, I was getting so sick of keeping it all in, that, I had no more room
left—so out it was spilling
In the only way—that my troubles knew how. For, I would not listen,
when they had said—NOW!
Until, it came to that day, when I walked and found my friend—with
whom they all talked.

'How come,' I asked Him 'did You know what to say, to make all of my
troubles decide to go away?'

'I just listened, accepting them for what they were, so, they just let go—of
trying to make you hear.
They just wanted to let you know how they feel. That the problems they
had, for them, they were real.
I'm so happy—now that you're feeling well. To feel that sick—must have
felt like hell!
So, now that you're better, we can go have some fun. Lets go play in the
park, see how far we can run
Or, go to the beach and splash in the sea. I am so happy that you came to
visit me.'

'Oh, by the way.' I say. 'I nearly forgot to ask. Is it true that you dance in
the dark and wear a mask?'

Laughing, with me, He took my hand and we danced—happily.

'We can dance anytime we want.' That's what He said to me.

'And, this face is the only one I've got.' As we looked into the mirror.
'So, if you listen to all you hear,
You'll get sick—with your own terror!'

UNTIL I RETURN

74

Your love, Is All I Need

Why does my ego put up a fight? Why does he struggle at all?
Does he not know that I will win, because, pride comes before a fall?
He keeps popping into my head. At times, when he hasn't been invited,
Telling me that I need so much stuff, and, he really gets so excited!
That, sometimes, I fall in to his trap, and think, that he must be right.
Especially, when all around me, are temptations that he puts in my sight.

There's brand new cars, houses and holiday, T.V.'s. stereos and computers.
Then, there's clothes and shoes, toys and booze, makeup, perfume, and a
few tours
Around the world in a big jet plane. But, why stop there? Lets rocket
into space!
Fly up to the stars. Maybe, even go to Mars! I could have a meteor race!
I could even visit the Man in the Moon! My ego is flying so high!
I sit down and look all around. Then, let out a huge big sigh!

For, in the end, I have it all. It's right in front of my face.
It's under my nose and in my hair. But, I live at such a fast pace,
That, I don't notice what's under my feet. I could even be sitting on it!
There's something in my eye, and, I don't know why, my heart it flutters a bit.
I look up to the sky. The moon is full, the stars are shiny and bright.
The Heavens are gazing down on me. It is such a beautiful night.

Sitting in my garden, thinking to myself, I thank God, for all that he
gives me.
He wakes me up with sunlight. He bathes me in the sea.
Everything, that, I need to live a happy life, is placed gently at my feet.
And, every now and then, without me even asking, He will leave me a treat.
All I have to do is pick it up and thank God, from the bottom of my heart.
And, tell my ego to go take a hike, because, when from this world I part—

All the struggle that I make to satisfy my ego, with all his worldly ways,
I ask 'will it be worth it?' For, in this world—it all stays.
I get down on my knees and pray to God, that, I will always see
That I came in to this world, with Your love—unencumbered and free,
To live my life, guided by You, with Your love deep down inside my
heart.
And, that's the way I'll leave this world—with Your love—when I finally
depart.

75

The World is Your Stage

I'd always thought I was in control.
That I had the leading role.
But, when the final curtain came down.
I felt so sad, as I changed my gown.

My emotions took over. They made such a mess.
They all disagreed—on how I should dress!
To reveal all, or, to stay covered up?
It was such a dilemma. They would not shut up!

They partied on—through the darkest night.
When I woke in the morning—what a terrible sight!
Bedraggled and dazed—I struggled through the day.
Then, a long lost stranger—passed by my way.

He said, 'The world is your oyster, for you to explore.
Be proud of your role today, for, there will be more.
Your parts will be varied—variety being the spice of life—
A baby, a child, a teenager, a husband, or a wife?

Whether playing the lead, or playing the fool,
Always try to remember the simple rule—
Enjoy each day, each moment, as if it were your last.
For, every moment in the present—soon becomes your past.

Your live performance may be repeated, but, is never the same.
There is a beginning and an end to this game.
You can role the dice, and choose to move,
Or, play the same record—get stuck in the groove.
Ride the rollercoaster, have fun at the fair.
Believe you are invincible. Accept every dare.

But, at the end of the day, when the curtain comes down.
Will you be wearing the mask of a clown?
Or, will you be playing your most important role?
The one that has given you—the freedom of your soul.'

76

No Escape

I live in a land called Australia.

It may seem far away

But, I see You on my T.V. screen

Almost every day.

I pick up a book, and,

Turn a page, or two.

But, 'Oh my God!'

You, are in there too!

Everywhere I turn and look

You're always in my face.

Maybe, You are even

Floating in outer space!

Knowing that You're all around

Watching every move I make,

I'll try to listen closely.

More notice, of You, I'll take.

For, innocently, I walk around and

Down the black hole—I gape.

And, ultimately, in the end

There is no escape!

77

Soldiering On

Take the good with the bad, the bad with the good.
Try not to tempt fate. Knock on wood.
Don't walk under ladders. Watch out for the black cat.
We're in for the ride of a lifetime—hold on to your hat!

So much to say, yet, it all says very little.
Life, seems to be, just one big riddle!
By the time you work it all out, it's getting very late.
Most of us are leading a life—that we really hate!

We've counted our chickens—before they've hatched!
We've picked up bad habits—to which we've become attached!
We did not look before we leapt and, got stuck in the mud!
Picked ourselves up, dusted ourselves down, and got covered in crud!

Yet, through it all, we soldiered on—believing it would get better.
Some of us got caught up in the storm—and just got a lot wetter!
We dribbled on, not caring, not looking where we were going.
Not taking any notice, or nurturing, the seeds we were sewing

Until, life finally turned around and bit us on the bum!
For, by then, it had had enough and decided, to the party, not to come.
It had got dressed up, but, there was nowhere to go.
So, it decided—to give up the ghost—have some fun in the snow.

The spirit was still willing,
Yet, we were as cold as ice.
As the earth—we departed,
We were as quiet as mice!

78

One Day

One day, when I'm not a baby any more
I won't cry. I'll be a big person. Go to the big toilet. Eat with a knife and
fork
And sit at the big table.
I can't wait till I'm able.
I'll be so clever and grown up.

One day, when I start school
I'll be a big kid. I'll draw and paint, and learn to read and write.
I'll stop sucking my thumb.
I won't miss my mum.

One day, when I grow up.
I'll be just like you. A doctor, a nurse, a dad, a mum.
A lawyer, a banker.
Tra la la la ho hum.

One day, when I get to high school
I won't be a little kid anymore. I'll make my own decisions
I'll be a teenager—ye ha!
I won't have to listen
To all their 'blah, blah, blah.'

One day, when these adults get off my case
I'll be able to concentrate on what needs to be faced. Decisions, exams,
TEE, Tafe, Uni, what career.
I've got to be strong
And hide my fear.

One day, when I go to college
I'll be respected for my choices. I'll be bigger and better and earn more
money.
I'm not gonna get flushed down the dunny!
Hey, that's kind of funny!

One day, when I start work
I'll earn lots of money, and, I'll be envied and admired.
I'll travel high places. Meet new faces.
Drive fast cars
Venus will meet Mars!

One day, when I get married
I'll take care of my partner. Give them my heart—right from the start.
Trust them, love them and share with them.
Not use and abuse them.
No way—will we ever part.

One day, when I have children
My life will be complete. I'll play and have fun. Take time and watch
them run.
I'll always listen and never refuse them.
'Hey, get out of the kitchen and that's my seat.'
'Whoa, who turned on the heat?'

One day, when the children grow up
Then, I'll be free to do all the things I want to, for me.
I'll take time to smell the flowers.
To draw. To paint. To sing a song
To take a journey.
But, right now,
I don't have any spare hours.

One day, when I'm a grandparent
I'll spend more time with the grandchildren
I'll make up for all the times I was too busy for mine.
I'll read them books and take them out and about.
I'll give them hugs.
I won't scream and shout.
But, sorry, not now. I have no patience, and no time.

One day, when I retire
I'll tour around the world. I'll see all the things I've been saving up to do.
But, first, I have to buy a new car.
Get a comfy chair.
My savings will be stretched too far!
Maybe, I'll just watch it
On the T.V. show, you know!

One day, when I'm old and grey
And I'm not sick and tired.
I'll try to remember if there was something I'd lost
Or
That, I just could not find.
Maybe
It's my mind?

One day

'Oh My God'

79

Stairway to Heaven

There is a stairway to Heaven, and, we must take the first step
To take His hand and trust in Him, that, everything will be alright.
'Faith will grow inside you, as you start to climb with Me.
I'll be your strength, beside you, as you face your darkest night.'

His promises, He keeps to us, as we learn to walk with Him.
We take a step, then, we may fall. But, we try and try again.
He lifts us up and says to us—'Maybe, you're ready for a nap,
For you are only a baby yet, so, let's rest and our strength regain.'

As we gain more confidence, we have no fear and run ahead.
We take a leap, then jump right in—no matter what we face!
He stands at the bottom of the slide, saying, 'I'll catch you if you fall.'
He pushes us on the swings, and joins in the three legged race.

We think we are invincible. We have no fear of what the future may bring.
For, we are young and they are old, we've a lifetime ahead of us yet.
Being young and foolish we rush, like fools, straight in. We dance and sing,
And hide our fears. We feel like we're number one. Then, Him, we forget.

We rush through life, find a husband or wife, a house and kids,
A car, a bike, a job we don't like, and fight with each other too.
And, all the time You are right there, watching and waiting.
For, You know there will come a time when, maybe, we'll remember You.

Then, one day, the step we take—that we think has taken us to the top—
Crumbles underneath us and, as we fall amongst the rubble,
We can choose to cling on desperately to all that we have acquired.
Or, sit down, turn around and ask, 'Is there is a way out of this trouble?'

'There is a way, but, first you must learn to walk—all over again.
To get down on your knees, and learn to climb the steps—one by one.
To ask for help and guidance and to take a rest on every step.
For, on the way up the stairway, you can walk but never run.

For these are the steps of life. There's a lesson on every one.
So take My hand, have faith and trust, that I'll be there.
To hold you when you're resting. To push you to do your best.
To be your guide when, you are so tired that, your eyes cannot see the stair.

For, at the top, you will find the climb was worth all the effort.
Because, what you see up there is a gift that is worth receiving.
It's waiting there, for you, to open. It's filled with so much love.
It's your reward for climbing, with Me, the Stairway to Heaven.'

80

On the Road with You

Life is really an open road
I see, as I drive in my car.
Do I look through tinted windows,
Or see things as they really are?
Can I see the beauty in all things
That I purvey on this earth,
The creations of my past,
The genesis of my souls birth?
Or, is it destroyed by the
Intelligence of my mind,
Seeking to control, to overwhelm,
Destroy the simplicity of all that I find?

Will I arrive at my destination,
Collect a few bumps along the way?
Will I listen to Your directions?
Will I try to have my say?
Make a detour? Lose my way?
Arrive at the end of my journey too soon?
Forget to enjoy the scenery?
As I ride safely within my cocoon.
Or, will it be one great adventure?
A magical rollercoaster ride,
With twists and turns, roundabouts and lights,
Stop signs, and access denied?

A journey, full of surprises,
That I am traveling with You.

An adventure of a lifetime,
To love and to live, enjoying the view.

As we travel down the road,
With the windows open wide,
Absorbing the beauty of this earth.

I really should enjoy the ride!